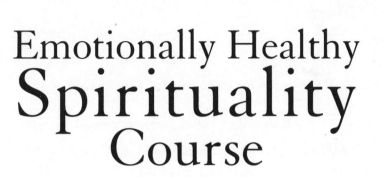

Emotionally Healthy
Spirituality
Course

WORKBOOK

Resources by Pete and/or Geri Scazzero

Emotionally Healthy Spirituality (book)

Emotionally Healthy Spirituality Course (workbook and DVD)

Emotionally Healthy Spirituality Church-Wide Initiative

Emotionally Healthy Spirituality Day by Day

The Emotionally Healthy Church

The Emotionally Healthy Woman (book, workbook, and DVD)

The Emotionally Healthy Leader (coming spring 2015)

Emotionally Healthy
Spirituality
Course

IT'S IMPOSSIBLE *to be* SPIRITUALLY MATURE,
WHILE REMAINING EMOTIONALLY IMMATURE

Peter & Geri Scazzero

ZONDERVAN®
.com

ZONDERVAN

Emotionally Healthy Spirituality Course Workbook
Copyright © 2008, 2014 by Peter L. and Geri Scazzero

This title is also available as a Zondervan ebook. Visit www.zondervan.com/ebooks.

Requests for information should be addressed to:

Zondervan, 3900 Sparks Dr. SE, Grand Rapids, Michigan 49546

ISBN 978-0-310-88253-4

Cover photo: Shutterstock® / © leonello calvetti
Author photos: Orlando Suazo
Interior illustration: 123RF® / Ion Popa
Interior design: Beth Shagene

First Printing May 2014 / Printed in the United States of America

Jul-18-2014

28102_CRC_1405

Contents

About the Authors

Geri Scazzero is the cofounder of New Life Fellowship Church in Queens, New York, where she serves on staff as a trainer in marriage and spiritual formation. Geri is also a popular conference speaker for church leaders, married couples, and women's groups, both in North America and internationally. She is the author of *The Emotionally Healthy Woman* and *The Emotionally Healthy Woman Workbook/DVD* and coauthor of the bestselling *Emotionally Healthy Spirituality Course* and *The Emotionally Healthy Skills 2.0* curriculum. Connect with Geri on Facebook (www.facebook.com/GeriScazzero).

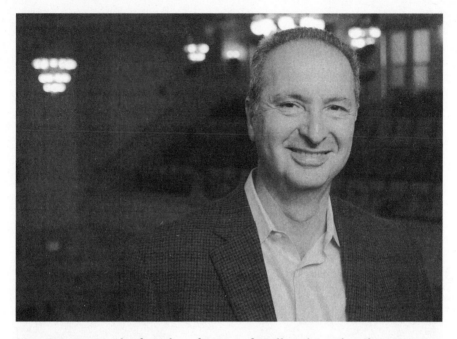

Pete Scazzero is the founder of New Life Fellowship Church in Queens, New York, a large, multiracial church with more than seventy-three countries represented. After serving as senior pastor for twenty-six years, Pete now serves as a teaching pastor/pastor at large. He is the author of two bestselling books — *The Emotionally Healthy Church* and *Emotionally Healthy Spirituality*. He is also the author of *The EHS Course* and *Emotionally Healthy Spirituality Day by Day*.

Pete and Geri are the founders of Emotionally Healthy Spirituality, a groundbreaking ministry that equips churches in a deep, beneath-the-surface spiritual formation paradigm that integrates emotional health and contemplative spirituality. They have four lovely daughters. For more information, visit emotionallyhealthy.org or connect with Pete on Facebook or Twitter @petescazzero.

Introduction

The goal of this workbook, along with its companion resources — the *Emotionally Healthy Spirituality Course* video, the *Emotionally Healthy Spirituality* book, and the *Emotionally Healthy Spirituality Day by Day* devotional — is to help you implement the biblical truths and principles found in the bestselling book *Emotionally Healthy Spirituality*. The thesis we are attempting to unpack is simple yet far-reaching:

> *Emotional health and contemplative spirituality, when interwoven together, offer nothing short of a spiritual revolution, transforming the hidden places deep beneath the surface of our lives.*

Each of the eight different principles explored in these sessions could easily have been expanded into its own workbook. The video and workbook are intended to serve only as an introduction into a life with God that goes beyond "tip of the iceberg spirituality" into transformation through Christ that touches the depth of your being. In fact, the implementation of these pathways will involve the rest of your life. The only condition is that you follow God, like Abraham, into the unknown (Hebrews 11:8).

How to Use This Workbook

Before Session 1

- Purchase the *Emotionally Healthy Spirituality* book, *Emotionally Healthy Spirituality Day by Day*, and this workbook.

- Read chapters 1 – 3 of the *Emotionally Healthy Spirituality* book. If you have limited time, simply read chapter 1.

- A brief video that introduces how to use *Emotionally Healthy Spirituality Day by Day* can be found on the *EHS Course* DVD, at www.emotionallyhealthy.org/ehscourse, or on YouTube.

Throughout the Study

- Though the temptation may be great to spend multiple weeks per session, try your best to adopt a *one meeting/one topic* pace. The workbook is ideally used as a broad introduction to all the concepts as an integrated whole. Working through *all* the topics together will enable you to better incorporate this material into your life. You can certainly revisit any of the sessions later, but initially please try to finish each session in one 90-minute meeting.

- Before each group meeting, you are strongly encouraged to read the chapters from the *Emotionally Healthy Spirituality* book that correspond with each session in this workbook. You are also encouraged to read the devotionals found in *Emotionally Healthy Spirituality Day by Day* during the week that follows the study.

- Each session is divided into six sections:
  - Introduction(also on the video)
  - Growing Connected
  - Video Presentation
  - Group Discussion (Starters and Bible Study)
  - Application and Closing Prayer
  - Between-Sessions Personal Study

  Space is provided throughout for you to record your responses, questions, or other insights that God may be bringing to you during your meeting time as well as during your personal study time between meetings.

- The Leader's Guide found in the back of this workbook provides extremely helpful information to supplement the studies. We especially encourage the leaders/facilitators of groups to avail themselves of this valuable material, but if you are using this workbook on your own, it will also serve you.

Suggested Guidelines
for the Group

Observe Confidentiality

In order to create an environment that is safe for open and honest participation, please limit your sharing to your own personal experiences. In addition, anything personal shared within the group should not be repeated outside of the group.

Speak for Yourself

Use "I" statements as often as possible. We are only experts on ourselves.

Respect Others

Be brief in your sharing, remaining mindful that there are time limitations and others may want to share.

Turn to Wonder

If you feel judgmental or defensive when someone else is sharing, ask yourself: *I wonder what brought him/her to this belief? I wonder what he/she is feeling right now? I wonder what my reaction teaches me about myself?*

Punctuality

Resolve to begin on time and end on time.

Be Prepared

To get the most out of your time together, we highly recommend that you read the chapters in *Emotionally Healthy Spirituality* that correspond with each session. Please also bring your Bible and workbook with you to each meeting.

Silence

It is okay to have silence between responses as the group shares, giving members the opportunity to reflect. Remember, there is no pressure to share.

The Problem of Emotionally Unhealthy Spirituality

(90+ MINUTES)

Before your first group meeting, read chapters 1 – 3 of the *Emotionally Healthy Spirituality* book.

Introduction

Emotional health and spiritual maturity cannot be separated. It is impossible to be spiritually mature while remaining emotionally immature. We know. We tried unsuccessfully for years.

When we ignore the emotional component of our lives, we move through the motions of Christian disciplines, activities, and behaviors, but deeply rooted behavioral patterns from our pasts continue to hinder us from an authentic life of maturity in Christ.

We often neglect to reflect on what is going on inside us and around us (emotional health) and are too busy to slow down to be with God (contemplative spirituality).[1] As a result, we run the high risk of remaining stuck as spiritual infants, failing to develop into spiritually/emotionally mature adults in Christ.

Jay, one of our church members, described it best: "I was a Christian for twenty-two years. But instead of being a twenty-two-year-old Christian, I was a one-year-old Christian twenty-two times! I just kept doing the same things over and over and over again."

Growing Connected (10 minutes)

1. Share your name, what you hope to get out of the group, and a few words about what makes you feel fully alive.

2. Have someone read aloud the "Suggested Guidelines for the Group" found right before Session 1.

VIDEO: The Problem of Emotionally Unhealthy Spirituality (20 minutes)

Watch the video segment for Session 1. Use the space provided to note anything that stands out to you.

NOTES

Group Discussion (45 minutes)

Starters (10 minutes)

3. **Two-Minute Takeaway:** What impacted you most about the video teaching for this session?

4. The following are the top ten symptoms of emotionally *unhealthy* spirituality. Take turns as a group reading the list aloud. Then share the one symptom that is most relevant in your life today.

   1. **Using God to run from God**
      (*Example:* My prayers are usually about God doing my will, not me surrendering to his.)

   2. **Ignoring the emotions of anger, sadness, and fear**
      (*Example:* I am rarely honest with myself and/or others about the feelings, hurts, and pains beneath the surface of my life.)

   3. **Dying to the wrong things**
      (*Example:* I tend to deny healthy, God-given desires and pleasures of life such as friendships, joy, music, beauty, laughter, and nature. At the same time, I find it difficult to die to my self-protectiveness, defensiveness, lack of vulnerability, and judgmentalism.)

   4. **Denying the past's impact on the present**
      (*Example:* I rarely consider how my family of origin and significant people/events from my past have shaped my present.)

   5. **Dividing life into "secular" and "sacred" compartments**
      (*Example:* I easily compartmentalize God to "Christian activities" while usually forgetting about him when I am working, shopping, studying, or recreating.)

   6. **Doing for God instead of being with God**
      (*Example:* I tend to evaluate my spirituality based on how much I am doing for God.)

   7. **Spiritualizing away conflict**
      (*Example:* I usually miss out on true peace by smoothing over disagreements, burying tensions, and avoiding conflict, rather than disrupting false peace as Jesus did.)

   8. **Covering over brokenness, weakness, and failure**
      (*Example:* I have a hard time speaking freely about my weaknesses, failures, and mistakes.)

   9. **Living without limits**
      (*Example:* Those close to me would say that I often "try to do it all" or "bite off more than I can chew.")

10. Judging the spiritual journeys of others
(*Example:* I often find myself occupied and bothered by the faults of those around me.)

Bible Study: 1 Samuel 15:7 – 24 (35 minutes)

Have a volunteer(s) read the introductory paragraph and Scripture passage, and then discuss the questions that follow.

Saul, king of Israel, was instructed by God to fight and completely destroy the Amalekites. He succumbed, however, to the wishes of his fighting men and did only part of God's will due to a lack of self-awareness (emotional health) and attentiveness toward God (contemplation). Read 1 Samuel 15:7 – 24.

> [7] Then Saul attacked the Amalekites all the way from Havilah to Shur, near the eastern border of Egypt. [8] He took Agag king of the Amalekites alive, and all his people he totally destroyed with the sword. [9] But Saul and the army spared Agag and the best of the sheep and cattle, the fat calves and lambs — everything that was good. These they were unwilling to destroy completely, but everything that was despised and weak they totally destroyed.
>
> [10] Then the word of the LORD came to Samuel: [11] "I regret that I have made Saul king, because he has turned away from me and has not carried out my instructions." Samuel was angry, and he cried out to the LORD all that night.
>
> [12] Early in the morning Samuel got up and went to meet Saul, but he was told, "Saul has gone to Carmel. There he has set up a monument in his own honor and has turned and gone on down to Gilgal."
>
> [13] When Samuel reached him, Saul said, "The LORD bless you! I have carried out the LORD's instructions."
>
> [14] But Samuel said, "What then is this bleating of sheep in my ears? What is this lowing of cattle that I hear?"

[15] Saul answered, "The soldiers brought them from the Amalekites; they spared the best of the sheep and cattle to sacrifice to the LORD your God, but we totally destroyed the rest."

[16] "Enough!" Samuel said to Saul. "Let me tell you what the LORD said to me last night."

"Tell me," Saul replied.

[17] Samuel said, "Although you were once small in your own eyes, did you not become the head of the tribes of Israel? The LORD anointed you king over Israel. [18] And he sent you on a mission, saying, 'Go and completely destroy those wicked people, the Amalekites; wage war against them until you have wiped them out.' [19] Why did you not obey the LORD? Why did you pounce on the plunder and do evil in the eyes of the LORD?"

[20] "But I did obey the LORD," Saul said. "I went on the mission the LORD assigned me. I completely destroyed the Amalekites and brought back Agag their king. [21] The soldiers took sheep and cattle from the plunder, the best of what was devoted to God, in order to sacrifice them to the LORD your God at Gilgal."

[22] But Samuel replied: "Does the LORD delight in burnt offerings and sacrifices as much as in obeying the LORD? To obey is better than sacrifice, and to heed is better than the fat of rams.

[23] For rebellion is like the sin of divination, and arrogance like the evil of idolatry. Because you have rejected the word of the LORD, he has rejected you as king."

[24] Then Saul said to Samuel, "I have sinned. I violated the LORD's command and your instructions. I was afraid of the men and so I gave in to them."

5. Verse 11 describes God's and Samuel's responses to Saul's actions. What about their responses impacts you?

How does this differ from Saul's response in verses 12 – 13?

6. What might have been going on beneath the surface of Saul's life (ice-berg) that he was unaware of?

7. Reread verses 22 – 23. Describe in your own words how Samuel explains Saul's disobedience.

8. What are some examples of how we go through the motions of making "burnt offerings" and "sacrifices" rather than obeying the word of the Lord?

9. Note the seriousness of verse 23a. What positive step(s) could Saul have taken to become aware of his own iceberg and hear God in his situation? What might be one positive step for you?

In what ways can you relate, or not relate, to Saul?

Application and Closing Prayer (15 minutes)

Answer the following application questions on your own and then, as a group, close the session in prayer.

Not only was Saul unaware of what was going on inside of him (emotional health), he also did not cultivate a contemplative life with God (as David did). His "doing" for God did not flow from his "being" with God.

In the same way, our "doing" for Jesus must flow from our "being" with him. Far too often, we live vicariously off other people's spirituality and relate to God while busily "on the run."

10. What challenges keep you from slowing down your life to be with God?

11. The diagram below provides an illustration of a spiritual life where our activity (i.e., our doing) is out of balance with our contemplative life (i.e., our inner life with Jesus).

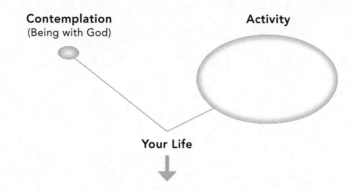

Now, using two circles like the ones in the diagram, draw your own diagram to illustrate how your activities (your doing) balance with your contemplative life (your being with God).[2]

12. The remainder of the workbook will address ways we can make changes in our lives. At this point, what might be one or two simple decisions that you can make toward taking a first step to slow down your life and balance your two circles?

Take a few minutes to pray together about what God has said to you during this first study.

Between-Sessions Personal Study

Read chapter 4 of the book *Emotionally Healthy Spirituality*, "Know Yourself That You May Know God." Use the space provided to note any insights or questions you might want to bring to the next group session.

Read Week 1 of the devotional *Emotionally Healthy Spirituality Day by Day*, "The Problem of Emotionally Unhealthy Spirituality." Use the space provided to answer the Questions to Consider and/or to journal your thoughts each day.

Day 1 Questions to Consider:

How would you describe "what is secondary" in your life, the thing that might be "blocking the way" to experiencing God?

How could you make more room in your life for silence in order to listen to God?

Day 2 Questions to Consider:

What internal or external storm might God be sending into your life as a sign that something is not right spiritually?

How do you hear the words of the apostle John today: "Do not love the world or anything in the world" (1 John 2:15)?

Day 3 Questions to Consider:

In what way(s) has God put your life or plans "out of joint" so that you might depend on him?

What might be one way your "busyness" blocks you from listening and communing with the living God?

Day 4 Questions to Consider:

What things are "worrying" and "upsetting" you as you begin this day?

What are you angry about today? Sad about? Afraid of? Pour out your responses before God, trusting in him as David did.

Day 5 Questions to Consider:

What is one step you can take today to slow down and live more attentively to the voice of Jesus?

How might brokenness or weakness in your life today present an opportunity for God's power to be demonstrated?

Know Yourself That You May Know God

(90 MINUTES)

Introduction

Self-awareness is intricately related to our relationship with God. In fact, the challenge of Scripture to shed our old "false" self in order to live authentically in our new "true" self strikes at the very core of true spirituality.

In AD 500, Augustine wrote in *Confessions*, "How can you draw close to God when you are far from your own self?" He prayed: "Grant, Lord, that I may know myself that I may know thee."

In 1530, John Calvin wrote in his opening of the *Institutes of the Christian Religion*: "Our wisdom ... consists almost entirely of two parts: the knowledge of God and of ourselves. But as these are connected together by many ties, it is not easy to determine which of the two precedes and gives birth to the other."

The vast majority of us go to our graves without knowing who we are. Without being fully aware of it, we live someone else's life, or at least someone else's expectations for us. This does violence to ourselves, to our relationship with God, and ultimately to others.

Growing Connected (12 minutes)

1. Describe your dream job. (Depending on group size, you'll have at most a couple of minutes to share.)

VIDEO: Know Yourself That You May Know God
(13 minutes)

Watch the video segment for Session 2. Use the space provided to note anything that stands out to you.

NOTES

Group Discussion (50 minutes)

Starters (15 minutes)

2. **Two-Minute Takeaway:** What impacted you most about the video teaching for this session?

Have a volunteer read the following paragraphs aloud; then take about 7 minutes to complete question 3 on your own before answering question 4 as a group.

The journey of genuine transformation to emotionally healthy spirituality begins with a commitment to allow yourself to feel. Feelings are an essential part of our humanity and unique personhood as men and women created in God's image. Scripture reveals God as an emotional being who feels as a person. Having been created in his image, we also are created with the gift to feel and experience emotions. Some of us may have learned that feelings are not to be trusted; that they are dangerous and can lead us away from God's will for us.

While it is true that we are not to be led by our emotions, they do serve a critical function in our discipleship and discernment of God's will.

There are hundreds of emotions, each with their variations, blends, and nuances. Researchers have classified them into eight main families as shown in the following question.

3. Choose four questions from the following list and journal your answers in the space provided. If you start journaling and find that there is a lot to write about on one particular feeling, then simply stay with it for the entire seven minutes.

• What are you angry about?

• What are you sad about?

• What are you fearful about? (health, finances, family, work, future, etc.)

- What are you mad about? (past, present, etc.)

- What are you enjoying and glad about?

- What (whom) do you love?

- What are you surprised by?

- What disgusts you?

4. What was it like to journal your feelings?

Bible Study: 1 Samuel 17:26 – 45 (35 minutes)

Have a volunteer(s) read the introductory paragraph and Scripture passage, and then discuss the questions that follow.

In this famous story, the army of Israel faced the great army of the Philistines. For forty days, the Philistine hero Goliath, described as nine feet tall and dressed in powerful weaponry, challenged any Israelite soldier to come out and fight him. When the Israelites saw him, however, "they all fled from him in great fear" (1 Samuel 17:24). We pick up the story after David hears, for the first time, Goliath's humiliating challenge to Israel's army. Read 1 Samuel 17:26 – 45.

> 26 David asked the men standing near him, "What will be done for the man who kills this Philistine and removes this disgrace from Israel? Who is this uncircumcised Philistine that he should defy the armies of the living God?"
>
> 27 They repeated to him what they had been saying and told him, "This is what will be done for the man who kills him."
>
> 28 When Eliab, David's oldest brother, heard him speaking with the men, he burned with anger at him and asked, "Why have you come down here? And with whom did you leave those few sheep in the wilderness? I know how conceited you are and how wicked your heart is; you came down only to watch the battle."
>
> 29 "Now what have I done?" said David. "Can't I even speak?" 30 He then turned away to someone else and brought up the same matter,

and the men answered him as before. [31] What David said was over-heard and reported to Saul, and Saul sent for him.

[32] David said to Saul, "Let no one lose heart on account of this Philistine; your servant will go and fight him."

[33] Saul replied, "You are not able to go out against this Philistine and fight him; you are only a young man, and he has been a warrior from his youth."

[34] But David said to Saul, "Your servant has been keeping his father's sheep. When a lion or a bear came and carried off a sheep from the flock, [35] I went after it, struck it and rescued the sheep from its mouth. When it turned on me, I seized it by its hair, struck it and killed it. [36] Your servant has killed both the lion and the bear; this uncircumcised Philistine will be like one of them, because he has defied the armies of the living God. [37] The LORD who rescued me from the paw of the lion and the paw of the bear will rescue me from the hand of this Philistine."

Saul said to David, "Go, and the LORD be with you."

[38] Then Saul dressed David in his own tunic. He put a coat of armor on him and a bronze helmet on his head. [39] David fastened on his sword over the tunic and tried walking around, because he was not used to them.

"I cannot go in these," he said to Saul, "because I am not used to them." So he took them off. [40] Then he took his staff in his hand, chose five smooth stones from the stream, put them in the pouch of his shepherd's bag and, with his sling in his hand, approached the Philistine.

[41] Meanwhile, the Philistine, with his shield bearer in front of him, kept coming closer to David. [42] He looked David over and saw that he was little more than a boy, glowing with health and handsome, and he despised him. [43] He said to David, "Am I a dog, that you come at me with sticks?" And the Philistine cursed David by his gods. [44] "Come here," he said, "and I'll give your flesh to the birds and the wild animals!"

[45] David said to the Philistine, "You come against me with sword and spear and javelin, but I come against you in the name of the LORD Almighty, the God of the armies of Israel, whom you have defied."

5. In your own words, what question does David ask after hearing Goliath's challenge (v. 26)?

6. What are some of the challenges, accusations, and messages David receives from the people around him?

   • From his own family (v. 28)

   • From Saul (vv. 33, 38)

   • From Goliath (vv. 41 – 45)

7. What feelings might you be experiencing if you were David? For example, what feelings might you have toward your sibling? Toward a person in authority over you (Saul)? Toward Goliath?

8. How does David live out his true self against the powerful forces and pressures that seek to mold him into someone he is not?

9. David's ability to be true to himself in the midst of great trials and pressures is, in modern terminology, called *differentiation*. (See this session in the Leader's Guide for a fuller explanation.) If David had been less differentiated, how might he have responded to his brothers, Saul, and Goliath?

Application and Closing Prayer (15 minutes)

Answer the following application questions on your own and then, as a group, close the session in prayer.

10. What forces and pressures from circumstances and people cause you to shrink back in fear or "wear armor" that does not fit your true self?

11. Many of us are so unaccustomed to distinguishing our true self from our false self that it may seem difficult to know where to begin. Complete the following sentence, and then share it with your group as a first step:

    What I am beginning to realize about myself is ...

Conclude this session prayerfully asking that you may know yourself that you might know God.

Between-Sessions Personal Study

 Read chapter 5 of the book *Emotionally Healthy Spirituality*, "Going Back in Order to Go Forward." Use the space provided to note any insights or questions you might want to bring to the next group session.

 Read Week 2 of the devotional *Emotionally Healthy Spirituality Day by Day*, "Know Yourself So That You May Know God." Use the space provided to answer the Questions to Consider and/or to journal your thoughts each day.

Day 1 Questions to Consider:

What might be one specific way that you give in to expectations of others rather than being faithful to what Jesus has for you?

What might be one false layer or bandage God is inviting you to remove today?

Day 2 Questions to Consider:

What do you think might be one of your "birthright" gifts from God that has been ignored in your life?

Where do you see yourself on Bernard's list of the four degrees of love?

Day 3 Questions to Consider:

What impresses you most about the story of Anthony's life?

What temptation(s) or trials do you find yourself in today that God may be using as a furnace to help develop your interior life?

Day 4 Questions to Consider:

What would it look like to respect yourself in light of your God-given limits?

What is one area of your inner person that the fire of God's presence might want to burn away (*ex.*: selfishness, greed, bitterness, impatience)?

Day 5 Questions to Consider:

How might it change your day today if you were to cease looking for human approval and begin seeking only the approval of God?

In what area of your life might you be living as a chicken when God, in reality, has made you an eagle?

Going Back in Order to Go Forward

(90 MINUTES)

Introduction

Emotionally healthy spirituality involves embracing God's choice to birth us into a particular family, in a particular place, at a particular moment in history.

That choice to embrace our past grants us certain opportunities and gifts. It also hands us a certain amount of "emotional baggage" for our journey through life. For some of us this load is minimal; for others, it is a heavy burden to carry.

True spirituality frees us to live joyfully in the present. Living joyfully, however, requires going back in order to go forward. This process takes us to the very heart of spirituality and discipleship in the family of God — breaking free from the destructive sinful patterns of our past in order to live the life of love that God intends.

Growing Connected (10 minutes)

1. How would you describe the family atmosphere you grew up in? Try to use just a word or two (*ex.*: affirming, complaining, critical, approachable, angry, tense, cooperative, competitive, close, distant, fun, serious).

VIDEO: Going Back in Order to Go Forward (13 minutes)

Watch the video segment for Session 3. Use the space provided to note anything that stands out to you.

NOTES

Group Discussion (40 minutes)

Starters (10 minutes)

2. **Two-Minute Takeaway:** What impacted you most about the video teaching for this session?

3. Our need to go back in order to go forward can be summed up in two essential biblical truths:

   • The blessings and sins of our families going back two to three generations profoundly impact who we are today.

   • Discipleship requires putting off the sinful patterns of our family of origin and relearning how to do life God's way in God's family.

What is your greatest fear in looking back at your family of origin to discern unhealthy patterns and themes? Explain.

Bible Study: Genesis 50:15 – 21 (30 minutes)

After a volunteer reads the introductory paragraph, answer question 4. Then have another volunteer read the next paragraph and Scripture passage before discussing the remaining questions.

The "family" is an emotional system of two to four generations who move through life together in different places at different times. When we are born into families, we inherit their ways of relating, their values, and their ways of living in the world. (Adopted children inherit not only birth family traits but draw on traits from their adoptive family.) Your family's story and your individual story cannot be separated.

Joseph is an excellent example of that reality. He was born into a complex, blended family where his father Jacob, Jacob's two wives, two concubines, and their children, all lived under one roof. Joseph was Jacob's favored son. As a result, his brothers grew jealous, leading them to sell Joseph to a merchant who took him to Egypt. The brothers never expected to hear from Joseph again. After he was sold, Joseph's life became very difficult. For the next ten to thirteen years, Joseph lived first as a slave, and later, as a prisoner falsely accused of rape.

4. Imagine yourself in Joseph's shoes sitting in a prison cell without any hope of freedom. What thoughts, feelings, or doubts might you have about your family? About yourself? About God?

Through God's miraculous intervention, Joseph was pulled from the pit of prison and made the second most powerful person in Egypt. Later, when his brothers came to Egypt for food during a famine in Israel, Joseph invited them to return for their father and live in Egypt — which they gladly did. But after Jacob died, the brothers began to worry. Read Genesis 50:15 – 21.

> [15] When Joseph's brothers saw that their father was dead, they said, "What if Joseph holds a grudge against us and pays us back for all the wrongs we did to him?" [16] So they sent word to Joseph, saying, "Your father left these instructions before he died: [17] 'This is what you are to say to Joseph: I ask you to forgive your brothers the sins and the wrongs they committed in treating you so badly.' Now please forgive the sins of the servants of the God of your father." When their message came to him, Joseph wept.
>
> [18] His brothers then came and threw themselves down before him. "We are your slaves," they said.
>
> [19] But Joseph said to them, "Don't be afraid. Am I in the place of God? [20] You intended to harm me, but God intended it for good to accomplish what is now being done, the saving of many lives. [21] So then, don't be afraid. I will provide for you and your children." And he reassured them and spoke kindly to them.

5. What assumptions are the brothers making about Joseph?

6. Why do you think Joseph weeps (v. 17)?

7. Joseph chooses to break the "normal" way his family deals with hurt feelings and conflict by forgiving his brothers. How might you have responded if you were in Joseph's position? (Be sure to honestly put yourself in Joseph's shoes.)

8. Slowly, reread verses 19 – 21. Here we see Joseph's response to the enormous losses he experienced in his life. Carefully consider the different aspects of this response below. As you think about your own life story, which one speaks the most to you?

   • "Don't be afraid."
   • "Am I in the place of God?"
   • "You intended to harm me, but God intended it for good."

Application and Closing Prayer (25 minutes)

Complete question 9 on your own. Then answer questions 10 – 12 as a group before closing together in prayer.

9. Joseph had a rich sense of being part of his family of origin and how it had shaped his life — both good and bad. We must honestly face the truths about our family of origin as well.

   Prayerfully complete the chart on the following page even if you have done a similar exercise before. We often receive new insights when we ponder and reflect on our family's impact on us at different times.

   • List the life messages you received from each of your parents or caretakers. (*ex.*: Don't be weak. Education is everything. You must achieve to be loved. Don't be sad; things could be worse. Make a lot of money. Don't trust people; they will hurt you.)

- List any "earthquake" events that sent "aftershocks" into your extended family. (*ex.*: abuse, premature or sudden deaths/losses, divorces, shameful secrets revealed, etc.)

- Review the three separate boxes and summarize what messages about life/yourself/others you internalized. Then fill in the middle box, "Cumulative messages I received."

Father (Caretaker)   **Mother (Caretaker)**

Messages received about life:

Messages received about life:

"Earthquake" events in family history:

-
-
-

Cumulative messages I received:

-
-

10. Share with the group the message(s) you received.

11. How do these messages compare with messages about who you are and how life is to be lived in God's family?

12. What might be one specific message from your family of origin that God has revealed to you today that you want to change as part of your "hard work of discipleship"?

Paul prays in Ephesians 1:18 – 19 that we might know God's incomparably great power for us who believe. When we receive Jesus Christ, the person of the Holy Spirit comes to live inside of us. Pray for one another. Pray for yourself, asking God to transform you and that all of your life might be a blessing to others!

Between-Sessions Personal Study

Read chapter 6 of the book *Emotionally Healthy Spirituality*, "Journey through the Wall." Use the space provided to note any insights or questions you might want to bring to the next group session.

Read Week 3 of the devotional *Emotionally Healthy Spirituality Day by Day*, "Going Back in Order to Go Forward." Use the space provided to answer the Questions to Consider and/or to journal your thoughts each day.

Day 1 Questions to Consider:

What invitation might God be offering to you out of the failures and pain of your past?

What heavy "raft" might you be carrying as you seek to climb the mountains God has placed before you?

Day 2 Questions to Consider:

What false self are you struggling with that Christ wants you to die to, so that you can truly live?

What most impacts you from the story about Francis? How is God speaking to you through that?

Day 3 Questions to Consider:

What would it look like for you to surrender the pains of your past (mistakes, sins, setbacks, and disappointments) to God today?

What pains in your life are waiting to be acknowledged and grieved?

Day 4 Questions to Consider:

What space in the world (for which the past has prepared you) is waiting to be filled by you?

Can you name ways in which you learned the pain of others by suffering your own pain?

Day 5 Questions to Consider:

How might the words from Exodus 14:14 – 15 — "The LORD will fight for you, you need only to be still" and "move on" — apply to you today?

In Psalm 131:1, David prays: "I do not concern myself with great matters or things too wonderful for me." How do you hear these words?

Journey through the Wall

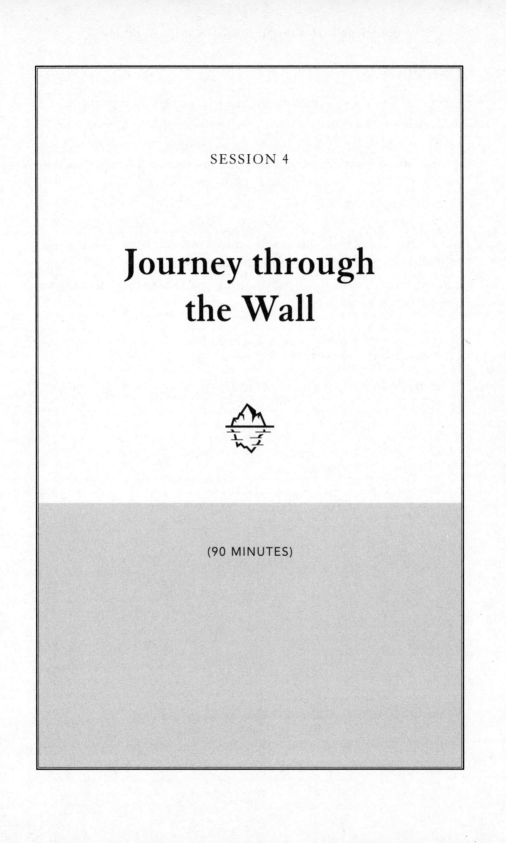

(90 MINUTES)

Introduction

Emotionally healthy spirituality requires that you go through the pain of the Wall — or, as the ancients called it, "the dark night of the soul." Just as a physical wall stops us from moving ahead, God sometimes stops us in our spiritual journey through a spiritual Wall in order to radically transform our character. Often, we are brought to the Wall by circumstances and crises beyond our control.

Regardless of how we get there, every follower of Jesus at some point will confront the Wall. Failure to understand and surrender to God's working in us at the Wall often results in great long-term pain, ongoing immaturity, and confusion. Receiving the gift of God in the Wall, however, transforms our lives forever.

Growing Connected (7 minutes)

1. In this season of your life, what is the greatest obstacle that you face? Explain.

VIDEO: Journey through the Wall (13 minutes)

Watch the video segment for Session 4. Use the space provided to note anything that stands out to you.

NOTES

Group Discussion (50 minutes)

Starters (15 minutes)

2. **Two-Minute Takeaway:** What impacted you most about the video teaching for this session?

Have a volunteer read the following excerpt from the book *Emotionally Healthy Spirituality* aloud before answering question 3.

For most of us, the Wall appears through a crisis that turns our world upside down. It comes, perhaps, through a divorce, a job loss, the death of a close friend or family member, a cancer diagnosis, a disillusioning church experience, a betrayal, a shattered dream, a wayward child, a car accident, an inability to get pregnant, a deep desire to marry that remains unfulfilled, a spiritual dryness or a loss of joy in our relationship with God. We question ourselves, God, and the church. We discover for the first time that our faith does not appear to "work." We have more questions than answers as the very foundation of our faith feels like it is on the line. We don't know where God is, what he is doing, where he is going, how he is getting us there, or when this will be over ... It (the Wall) is not simply a one-time event that we pass through and get beyond. It appears to be something we return to as part of our ongoing relationship with God.

(pp. 120 – 121)

3. If you have been through a Wall, briefly share one way it impacted you and your view of God.

Bible Study: Genesis 22:1 – 14 (35 minutes)

Have a volunteer(s) read the introductory paragraph and Scripture passage, and then discuss the questions that follow.

Abraham, in his earthly pilgrimage with God, appeared to go through a number of Walls. His greatest one, however, came when God asked him to do the unthinkable — to kill his only son Isaac. Read Genesis 22:1 – 14:

[1] Some time later God tested Abraham. He said to him, "Abraham!"

"Here I am," he replied.

[2] Then God said, "Take your son, your only son, whom you love — Isaac — and go to the region of Moriah. Sacrifice him there as a burnt offering on a mountain I will show you."

[3] Early the next morning Abraham got up and loaded his donkey. He took with him two of his servants and his son Isaac. When he had cut enough wood for the burnt offering, he set out for the place God had told him about. [4] On the third day Abraham looked up and saw the place in the distance. [5] He said to his servants, "Stay here with the donkey while I and the boy go over there. We will worship and then we will come back to you."

[6] Abraham took the wood for the burnt offering and placed it on his son Isaac, and he himself carried the fire and the knife. As the two of them went on together, [7] Isaac spoke up and said to his father Abraham, "Father?"

"Yes, my son?" Abraham replied.

"The fire and wood are here," Isaac said, "but where is the lamb for the burnt offering?"

[8] Abraham answered, "God himself will provide the lamb for the burnt offering, my son." And the two of them went on together.

[9] When they reached the place God had told him about, Abraham built an altar there and arranged the wood on it. He bound his son Isaac and laid him on the altar, on top of the wood. [10] Then he reached out his hand and took the knife to slay his son. [11] But the angel of the LORD called out to him from heaven, "Abraham! Abraham!"

"Here I am," he replied.

[12] "Do not lay a hand on the boy," he said. "Do not do anything to him. Now I know that you fear God, because you have not withheld from me your son, your only son."

[13] Abraham looked up and there in a thicket he saw a ram caught by its horns. He went over and took the ram and sacrificed it as a burnt offering instead of his son. [14] So Abraham called that place The LORD Will Provide. And to this day it is said, "On the mountain of the LORD it will be provided."

4. How would you hear the words in verse 2: "Take your son, your only son, whom you love ... sacrifice him"?

5. What aspects of "the dark night" might have been tormenting Abraham's soul as he bound his son Isaac and laid him on the altar? (*ex.:* weariness, sense of failure, defeat, emptiness, dryness, unbelief, guilt, disillusionment, abandonment by God)

6. In light of this story, how is your image of God challenged?

7. What are some possible reasons we have a hard time accepting and moving through Walls?

8. In order to grow in Christ, every believer must go through Walls, or "dark nights of the soul." This is God's way of rewiring and "purging our affections and passions" that we might delight in his love and enter into a richer, fuller communion with him. In this way he frees us from unhealthy attachments and idolatries of the world. How might this larger perspective serve as an encouragement to you today?

9. In light of how the story ends, what do you learn about God as Provider (v. 14)?

Application and Closing Prayer (20 minutes)

Take about 5 minutes to complete question 10 on your own. Then close in prayer, as specified.

10. When God takes us through a Wall, we are changed. The following are four primary characteristics of life found on the other side of the Wall.

    • A greater level of brokenness
    • A greater appreciation for holy unknowing (mystery)
    • A deeper ability to wait on God
    • A greater detachment (from the world)

    Journaling can be a powerful tool to help clarify areas of life where God desires to bring transformation. It illuminates what is going on inside of us. Few tools get us to the "issue beneath the issue" like journaling.

    Choose one characteristic from the above list where you sense God is seeking to work in you now. Use the space provided to journal your thoughts and feelings regarding how God is birthing something new in you and/or helping you shed incomplete or immature ideas about him.

End your time together in groups of two by sharing and praying for one another.

Between-Sessions Personal Study

Read chapter 7 of the book *Emotionally Healthy Spirituality*, "Enlarge Your Soul through Grief and Loss." Use the space provided to note any insights or questions you might want to bring to the next group session.

Read Week 4 of the devotional *Emotionally Healthy Spirituality Day by Day*, "Journey through the Wall." Use the space provided to answer the Questions to Consider and/or to journal your thoughts each day.

Day 1 Questions to Consider:

What does it mean for you to trust in the slow work of God today?

What treasures might there be in such "darkness" or difficulties in your own life today?

Day 2 Questions to Consider:

What might be some unhealthy attachments or "idols" God wants to remove from your life in order to lead you to deeper, richer communion with him?

What things or people are you rooting your identity in that God may want to dig up so that your identity might be replanted in him?

Day 3 Questions to Consider:

Have you experienced any "terrible" circumstances that (in time) actually turned out to be a rich blessing?

What words or phrases from the Richard Rohr quote most speak to you? Why?

Day 4 Questions to Consider:

How is God inviting you to wait on him today?

In your own words, speak to God about your willingness to go where he leads you. What joys and/or fears accompany your willingness?

Day 5 Questions to Consider:

What is one thing God might want you to unlearn today?

What words speak to you most from the prayer found in the midday/evening Office of Week 4? Why?

Enlarge Your Soul through Grief and Loss

(90 MINUTES)

Introduction

Loss is a place where self-knowledge and powerful transformation can happen — if we have the courage to participate fully in the process.

We all face many "deaths" within our lives. Our culture routinely interprets these losses and griefs as alien invasions and interruptions to our "normal" lives. The choice is whether these deaths will be terminal (crushing our spirit and life) or will open us up to new possibilities and depths of transformation in Christ.

Growing Connected (7 minutes)

1. As you were growing up, how did you deal with your disappointments? Give one example.

VIDEO: Enlarge Your Soul through Grief and Loss
(13 minutes)

Watch the video segment for Session 5. Use the space provided to note anything that stands out to you.

NOTES

Group Discussion (50 minutes)

Starters (15 minutes)

2. **Two-Minute Takeaway:** What impacted you most about the video teaching for this session?

3. Briefly share one loss you have experienced this past year. How has this loss impacted you?

Bible Study: Matthew 26:31 – 44 (35 minutes)

Have a volunteer(s) read the introductory paragraph and Scripture passage, and then discuss the questions that follow.

The end of Jesus' vibrant, popular, earthly life and ministry appeared to be an enormous loss to his disciples and followers. In this passage we will observe two very different approaches to that loss — the apostle Peter's and Jesus' himself. Read Matthew 26:31 – 44:

> [31] Then Jesus told them, "This very night you will all fall away on account of me, for it is written: 'I will strike the shepherd, and the sheep of the flock will be scattered.' [32] But after I have risen, I will go ahead of you into Galilee."
> [33] Peter replied, "Even if all fall away on account of you, I never will."
> [34] "Truly I tell you," Jesus answered, "this very night, before the rooster crows, you will disown me three times."
> [35] But Peter declared, "Even if I have to die with you, I will never disown you." And all the other disciples said the same.

³⁶ Then Jesus went with his disciples to a place called Gethsemane, and he said to them, "Sit here while I go over there and pray." ³⁷ He took Peter and the two sons of Zebedee along with him, and he began to be sorrowful and troubled. ³⁸ Then he said to them, "My soul is overwhelmed with sorrow to the point of death. Stay here and keep watch with me."

³⁹ Going a little farther, he fell with his face to the ground and prayed, "My Father, if it is possible, may this cup be taken from me. Yet not as I will, but as you will."

⁴⁰ Then he returned to his disciples and found them sleeping. "Couldn't you men keep watch with me for one hour?" he asked Peter. ⁴¹ "Watch and pray so that you will not fall into temptation. The spirit is willing, but the flesh is weak."

⁴² He went away a second time and prayed, "My Father, if it is not possible for this cup to be taken away unless I drink it, may your will be done."

⁴³ When he came back, he again found them sleeping, because their eyes were heavy. ⁴⁴ So he left them and went away once more and prayed the third time, saying the same thing.

4. Peter was deeply invested in Jesus and his kingdom, having left everything to follow him. What was Peter's response to Jesus' shocking prediction (vv. 31 – 36)?

5. Following is a list of common defenses we often use to protect ourselves from grief and loss. Checkmark the common defenses that Peter used to protect himself against the painful reality of Jesus' prediction:

☐ Denial

☐ Minimizing (admitting something is wrong but in such a way that it appears less serious than it actually is)

☐ Blaming others (or God)

☐ "Over-spiritualizing"

☐ Blaming oneself

☐ Rationalizing (offering excuses and justifications)

☐ Intellectualizing (giving analysis and theories to avoid personal awareness or difficult feelings)

☐ Distracting

☐ Becoming hostile

☐ Medicating (with unhealthy addictions or attachments to numb our
pain)

6. Based on the checklist in question 5, can you identify defenses you
tend to use when dealing with loss and setbacks, and why?

7. It is important for us to remember that Jesus was both fully human and
fully God. Spend a few moments focusing on Jesus in verses 36 – 41. In
contrast to the checklist in question 5, what were some of the ways he
dealt with and moved through his losses?

8. What about Jesus' example of grieving most speaks to you about
embracing your own grief and loss?

Application and Closing Prayer (20 minutes)

Answer the following application questions on your own and then, as a group, spend 5 – 10 minutes closing the session in prayer.

9. Using the chart that follows, choose two or three age ranges of your life, and write down your significant losses during those years.

GRIEF CHART

Age (in years)	Losses/Disappointments Experienced	Your Response at the Time
3–12		
13–18		
19–25		
26–40		
41+		

10. What was the experience of filling out the chart like for you? Did it reveal anything new to you? Explain.

11. One of the central messages of Christianity is that suffering and death bring resurrection and new life. Are there any losses you have not yet embraced where new life is still waiting to be birthed?

Pray together as a group regarding what is in your heart in response to this study.

Between-Sessions Personal Study

Read chapter 8 of the book *Emotionally Healthy Spirituality*, "Discover the Rhythms of the Daily Office and Sabbath." Use the space provided to note any insights or questions you might want to bring to the next group session.

Read Week 5 of the devotional *Emotionally Healthy Spirituality Day by Day*, "Enlarge Your Soul through Grief and Loss." Use the space provided to answer the Questions to Consider and/or to journal your thoughts each day.

Day 1 Questions to Consider:

What does it mean for you to pray, "Yet not as I will, but as you will"?

How can you see God enlarging your soul through your losses?

Day 2 Questions to Consider:

In what ways is God bringing you to your knees before him through difficulties and setbacks in your life today?

What about Horatio Spafford and his relationship with Christ moves you the most?

Day 3 Questions to Consider:

What "road closed" sign is before you today that may be God's way of redirecting you to something new?

Name one or two limits God has placed in your life today as a gift.

Day 4 Questions to Consider:

What might it mean for you to mature by entering the painful reality of your losses rather than avoiding them?

How would it change your prayer life to bring to God what is *actually* in you and not what you think *ought* to be in you?

Day 5 Questions to Consider:

In what way(s) are you tempted to spin or cover over your losses and miss God's deeper work in your interior?

How is God coming to you through the "mini-deaths" in your life now?

Discover the Rhythms of the Daily Office and Sabbath

(90 MINUTES)

Introduction

Many of us are eager to develop our relationship with God. The problem, however, is that we can't seem to stop long enough to be with him. And if we aren't busy, we feel guilty that we are wasting time and not being productive. It is like being addicted — not to drugs or alcohol — but to tasks, work, and doing.

But God is offering us a way to deeply root our lives in him. This can be found in two ancient disciplines going back thousands of years — the Daily Office and Sabbath. When placed inside present-day Christianity, the Daily Office and Sabbath are groundbreaking, countercultural acts that go against the grain of our fast-paced Western culture.

Stopping for the Daily Office and Sabbath is not meant to add another "to-do" to our already busy schedules. It is the resetting of our entire lives toward a new destination — God himself. These practices enable us to stay attuned to God's presence throughout our days and weeks.

Growing Connected (7 minutes)

1. What is one practice you do on a daily/weekly basis that helps you stay connected to God?

VIDEO: Discover the Rhythms of the Daily Office and Sabbath (13 minutes)

Watch the video segment for Session 6. Use the space provided to note anything that stands out to you.

NOTES

Group Discussion (50 minutes)

Starters (20 minutes)

2. **Two-Minute Takeaway:** What impacted you most about the video teaching for this session?

We now have the opportunity to experience this practice called the Daily Office. Have a volunteer read aloud the following instructions for the group exercise. Choose another volunteer to read the part of the facilitator for the exercise itself. Afterward, answer question 3 together.

- For the next 10 minutes, we are going to engage in what is called a Daily Office. An Office is a time to stop, slow down, center, and pause to be with Jesus.
- Notice there is silence for 1 minute at the beginning and conclusion of each Office.
- We will also pause for about 15 seconds between the readings/prayers.

- Take a minute and get an overview of the Scriptures we will be praying together. We will pray them aloud together. Watch for the facilitator's cue.

Daily Office

Facilitator *(read slowly, thoughtfully)***:** To begin, I invite you to close your eyes for a few moments. Step out of all your roles in life — father, mother, leader, employee, boss, student, friend, brother, sister, teacher. Right now, you are only a child of God. To prepare for this Daily Office, imagine God delighting in you as a parent delights in their child. He is eager to give you his undivided attention, his time. His eyes sparkle as he gazes upon your face. He is smiling and loving all over you. What are the words you would love to hear God say to you? Allow him to speak those words over you.

As Scripture instructs us to "be still and know that I am God" (Psalm 46:10 NRSV), so we will begin and end our time together with a minute of silence.

Silence (1 minute)

Opening Prayer

Facilitator: Let's read aloud together:
Together:

> Teach us to number our days,
>> that we may gain a heart of wisdom.
> A thousand years in your sight
>> are like a day that has just gone by,
>> or like a watch in the night.
> May the favor of the Lord our God rest on us;
>> establish the work of our hands for us —
>> yes, establish the work of our hands.

> *(Psalm 90:12, 4, 17)*

Pause (15 seconds)

Facilitator: Let's read aloud together:

Together:

> We wait in hope for the LORD;
> > he is our help and our shield.
> In him our hearts rejoice,
> > for we trust in his holy name.
> May your unfailing love be with us, LORD,
> > even as we put our hope in you.
>
> > *(Psalm 33:20 – 22)*

Pause (15 seconds)

Facilitator: Let's read aloud together:

Together:

> Our Father who is in heaven,
> Hallowed be Your name.
> Your kingdom come.
> Your will be done,
> > On earth as it is in heaven.
> Give us this day our daily bread.
> And forgive us our debts,
> > as we also have forgiven our debtors.
> And do not lead us into temptation,
> > but deliver us from evil.
> For Yours is the kingdom and the power and the glory forever.
> > Amen.
>
> > *(Matthew 6:9 – 14 NASB)*

Pause (15 seconds)

Concluding Prayer

Facilitator: Let's read aloud together:

Together: Lord, you say that "in repentance and rest is your salvation, in quietness and trust is your strength." Teach me to rest and trust in you throughout the remainder of this day. "Teach me your way, LORD, that I may rely on your faithfulness; give me an undivided heart that I may fear your name … For great is your love toward me" (Isaiah 30:15 and Psalm 86:11, 13).

Conclude with silence (1 minute)

3. As a group, briefly share your thoughts and feelings about this experience.

Bible Study: Daniel 6:6 – 10; Exodus 20:1 – 17 (30 minutes)

Have a volunteer(s) read the introductory paragraph and Daniel passage, and then answer questions 4 – 7. Then have a different volunteer read the Ten Commandments from Exodus 20:1 – 17 before answering question 8.

After being forcibly removed from his country and home, Daniel was given a prestigious education and high-level job in government. The pressure on him to conform to the worldly, pagan values of Babylon was great. The following example gives us insight into one of the secrets of his faithful devotion to God. Read Daniel 6:6 – 10.

[6] So these administrators and satraps went as a group to the king and said: "May King Darius live forever! [7] The royal administrators, prefects, satraps, advisers and governors have all agreed that the king should issue an edict and enforce the decree that anyone who prays to any god or human being during the next thirty days, except to you, Your Majesty, shall be thrown into the lions' den. [8] Now, Your Majesty, issue the decree and put it in writing so that it cannot be altered — in accordance with the law of the Medes and Persians, which cannot be repealed." [9] So King Darius put the decree in writing.

[10] Now when Daniel learned that the decree had been published, he went home to his upstairs room where the windows opened toward

Jerusalem. Three times a day he got down on his knees and prayed, giving thanks to his God, just as he had done before.

4. Reread verse 10 aloud. How do the words in this verse speak to you?

5. How do you think this practice anchored Daniel in God and enabled him to resist the great pressure he was facing?

6. What costs were involved for Daniel?

7. What are the greatest obstacles preventing you from stopping to be with God two or three times a day?

These are the Ten Commandments as recorded in Exodus 20:1 – 17:

¹ And God spoke all these words:
² "I am the LORD your God, who brought you out of Egypt, out of the land of slavery.
³ "You shall have no other gods before me.
⁴ "You shall not make for yourself an image in the form of anything

in heaven above or on the earth beneath or in the waters below. [5] You shall not bow down to them or worship them; for I, the LORD your God, am a jealous God, punishing the children for the sin of the parents to the third and fourth generation of those who hate me, [6] but showing love to a thousand generations of those who love me and keep my commandments.

[7] "You shall not misuse the name of the LORD your God, for the LORD will not hold anyone guiltless who misuses his name.

[8] "Remember the Sabbath day by keeping it holy. [9] Six days you shall labor and do all your work, [10] but the seventh day is a sabbath to the LORD your God. On it you shall not do any work, neither you, nor your son or daughter, nor your male or female servant, nor your animals, nor any foreigner residing in your towns. [11] For in six days the LORD made the heavens and the earth, the sea, and all that is in them, but he rested on the seventh day. Therefore the LORD blessed the Sabbath day and made it holy.

[12] "Honor your father and your mother, so that you may live long in the land the LORD your God is giving you.

[13] "You shall not murder.

[14] "You shall not commit adultery.

[15] "You shall not steal.

[16] "You shall not give false testimony against your neighbor.

[17] "You shall not covet your neighbor's house. You shall not covet your neighbor's wife, or his male or female servant, his ox or donkey, or anything that belongs to your neighbor."

8. Reread the fourth commandment in verses 8 – 11. Sabbath is engaging in a regular rhythm of stopping, resting, delighting, and contemplating God for a twenty-four hour block of time each week. What, if any, is your current practice around Sabbath-keeping?

Application and Closing Prayer (20 minutes)

Read the introductory material and answer the questions on your own, and then spend 10 minutes as a group closing in prayer.

Biblical Sabbaths have four foundational qualities that distinguish them from a "day off."

- **Stop:** "To stop" is built into the literal meaning of the Hebrew word. We have limits. God is on the throne running the world. We are called to let go and trust him.
- **Rest:** Once we stop, we are called to rest from our work and our "doings."
- **Delight:** We are to slow down so we can enjoy what we have been given.
- **Contemplate:** We are to ponder the love of God. Every Sabbath we taste the glorious eternal party that awaits us when we see him face to face (see Revelation 22:4).

Sabbath is like receiving the gift of a heavy snow day every week. Stores are closed. Roads are impassable. Suddenly you have the gift of a day to do whatever you want. You don't have any obligations, pressures, or responsibilities. You have permission to play, be with friends, take a nap, read a good book. Few of us would give ourselves a "no obligation day" very often. God does — every seventh day.

Think about it. He gives you over seven weeks (fifty-two days in all) of snow days every year!

9. What difference would it make in your life if you celebrated a Sabbath every week?

10. What questions, concerns, or fears do you have that keep you from making this practice a part of your weekly rhythm?

11. Journal a Response: Both the Daily Office and the Sabbath are concerned with a rhythm in our days and our weeks. In the space provided, take a few minutes to journal one small step you can take to begin to incorporate one of these two ancient disciplines.

Close in prayer together, committing your plan to God.

Between-Sessions Personal Study

Read chapter 9 of the book *Emotionally Healthy Spirituality*, "Grow into an Emotionally Mature Adult." Use the space provided to note any insights or questions you might want to bring to the next group session.

Read Week 6 of the devotional *Emotionally Healthy Spirituality Day by Day*, "Discover the Rhythms of the Daily Office and Sabbath." Use the space provided to answer the Questions to Consider and/or to journal your thoughts each day.

Day 1 Questions to Consider:

Pause and consider your day. What "seeds" from God might be coming to you that you don't want to miss?

How do you hear the invitation to "stop and surrender to God in trust" today?

Day 2 Questions to Consider:

When can you set aside some time for extended, uninterrupted silence to hear God?

How might you be busier than God requires?

Day 3 Questions to Consider:

What keeps you from silence?

How do the rhythms you see in nature (spring, summer, fall, winter, day, night) speak to you about the kind of rhythms you desire for your own life?

Day 4 Questions to Consider:

What is your greatest fear in stopping for a twenty-four-hour period each week?

How might Sabbath-keeping (for an entire twenty-four-hour period) or a Daily Office (a mini-Sabbath for a few minutes) provide for you a taste of eternity?

Day 5 Questions to Consider:

How will you allow God to lead you to the "quiet waters" of rest this week so that you experience his unconditional love and acceptance?

How might the truth that God doesn't want to use you, but to enjoy you, give you a vision for celebrating Sabbath?

Grow into an Emotionally Mature Adult

(90 MINUTES)

Introduction

The goal of the Christian life is to love well. Jesus was aware that true spirituality included not only loving God but also the skill of loving others maturely.

Growing into an emotionally mature Christian person includes experiencing each individual, ourselves included, as sacred, or as Martin Buber put it, as a "Thou" rather than an "It." Becoming emotionally mature requires learning, practicing, and integrating such skills as speaking respectfully, listening with empathy, negotiating conflict fairly, and uncovering the hidden expectations we have of others ... just to name a few.

As we will see in today's Bible study on the parable of the Good Samaritan, both self-respect and compassion for others are part of a life rooted in "I-Thou" relating.

Growing Connected (10 minutes)

1. As a group, brainstorm two lists (on a whiteboard, if one is available): qualities that describe emotional immaturity and qualities that describe emotional maturity. As you think about these qualities, consider how we treat/view ourselves and how we treat/view other people.

Emotional Immaturity	Emotional Maturity

VIDEO: Growing into an Emotionally Mature Adult
(13 minutes)

Watch the video segment for Session 7. Use the space provided to note anything that stands out to you.

NOTES

Group Discussion (40 minutes)

Starters (10 minutes)

2. **Two-Minute Takeaway:** What impacted you most about the video teaching for this session?

3. Why do you think we can be committed and "growing" in Christ and yet not be growing in our ability to be "prayerfully present" or loving toward others?

Bible Study: Luke 10:25 – 37 (30 minutes)

Have a volunteer(s) read the introductory paragraph and Scripture passage, and then discuss the questions that follow.

Who can hear a story on the news about someone getting mugged, robbed, stripped naked, and left for dead in an alleyway without being affected? These real-life stories also happened in the days of Jesus. And Jesus told a parable recorded in Luke 10:25 – 37 that imagines one such disturbing story — with an unusual twist.

25 On one occasion an expert in the law stood up to test Jesus. "Teacher," he asked, "what must I do to inherit eternal life?"

26 "What is written in the Law?" he replied. "How do you read it?"

27 He answered, " 'Love the Lord your God with all your heart and with all your soul and with all your strength and with all your mind'; and, 'Love your neighbor as yourself.' "

28 "You have answered correctly," Jesus replied. "Do this and you will live."

29 But he wanted to justify himself, so he asked Jesus, "And who is my neighbor?"

30 In reply Jesus said: "A man was going down from Jerusalem to Jericho, when he was attacked by robbers. They stripped him of his clothes, beat him and went away, leaving him half dead. 31 A priest happened to be going down the same road, and when he saw the man, he passed by on the other side. 32 So too, a Levite, when he came to the place and saw him, passed by on the other side. 33 But a Samaritan, as he traveled, came where the man was; and when he saw him, he took pity on him. 34 He went to him and bandaged his wounds, pouring on oil and wine. Then he put the man on his own donkey, brought him to an inn and took care of him. 35 The next day he took out two denarii and gave them to the innkeeper. 'Look after him,' he said, 'and when I return, I will reimburse you for any extra expense you may have.'

36 "Which of these three do you think was a neighbor to the man who fell into the hands of robbers?"

37 The expert in the law replied, "The one who had mercy on him." Jesus told him, "Go and do likewise."

4. According to Martin Buber, the great Jewish theologian, we treat people as an "It" when we use them as means to an end or as objects. We treat people as a "Thou," when we recognize each person as a separate human being made in God's image and treat them with dignity and respect.[3] If you were the priest or Levite, what are some of the reasons you may have passed by this man and treated him as an "It" instead of a "Thou"?

5. Look back at verses 31 – 33. What did the Samaritan see and feel that the priest and Levite did not?

6. On your own, journal your thoughts on the following questions for two minutes. Then have one or two volunteers share their responses.

   • Can you think of a time when you were seen in a negative light, treated as inferior, or passed over as invisible? How did it feel?

   • Who have you been taught not to see or to treat as an "It"?

7. Reread verses 33 – 36. The Samaritan's compassion led him to stop and help the hurting man. At the same time, how did he demonstrate self-respect and awareness of his limits?

8. What are some of your challenges when it comes to loving your neighbor and loving yourself?

9. In light of how God is coming to you through this study, how do you hear the words in verse 37 to "go and do likewise"?

Application[4] and Closing Prayer (25 minutes)

Read the introductory material and answer questions 10 and 11 on your own. Then answer question 12 and pray in groups of two or three.

One way of growing in the area of loving others well, and treating ourselves and others as a "Thou," is to understand how we manage our expectations in relationships.

EXPECTATIONS are ASSUMPTIONS about what someone SHOULD do. Every time we make an assumption about someone without checking it out, it is likely we are treating them as an "It" and not a "Thou." Why? We are jumping to conclusions without having checked out the assumption. Consider how you feel when someone is angry with you because you didn't fulfill their expectations, yet they never communicated this expectation to you. They simply assumed you should know.

Unmet and unclear expectations can create havoc in our places of employment, classrooms, friendships, dating relationships, marriages, sports teams, families, and churches. We expect other people to know what we want before we say it. The problem with most expectations is that they are:

- **Unconscious:** We may have expectations we're not even aware of until we are disappointed by someone.
- **Unrealistic:** We may develop unrealistic expectations by watching TV, movies, or other people/resources that give false impressions.
- **Unspoken:** We may have never told our spouse, friend, or employee what we expect, yet we are angry when our "expectations" are not met.
- **Un-agreed upon:** We may have had our own thoughts about what was expected, but those thoughts were never agreed upon by the other person.

10. Think of a recent, simple expectation that went unmet and made you angry or disappointed. (*Examples:* I expected my husband to accompany me to my office party this past weekend; I expected to socialize with members of my small group outside the meeting times; I expected my teenagers to put their dirty dishes in the dishwasher; I expected my boss to give me at least a 5 percent cost of living raise last year.) Write yours down.

11. Now compare that unmet expectation with the inventory questions below:
   - **Conscious:** Were you conscious (aware) you had this expectation?

- **Realistic:** Is the expectation realistic regarding the other person?

- **Spoken:** Have you clearly spoken the expectation to them or do you just think "they should know"?

- **Agreed upon:** Has the other person agreed to the expectation?

Remember this principle: Expectations are only valid when they have been mutually agreed upon. These are the expectations we have a right to expect.

12. Break into groups of two or three and respond to the following two questions:

- What did you discover about your expectations?

- What step(s) can you take to make your expectations conscious, spoken, realistic, and agreed upon so that you are relating in an "I-Thou" way?

Pray. Ask God to grant you the courage to make the changes you need in the way you relate to others; i.e., to love maturely by treating yourself and others as a "Thou" rather than an "It."

Between-Sessions Personal Study

 Read chapter 10 of the book *Emotionally Healthy Spirituality*, "Go the Next Step to Develop a 'Rule of Life.'" Use the space provided to note any insights or questions you might want to bring to the next group session.

 Read Week 7 of the devotional *Emotionally Healthy Spirituality Day by Day*, "Grow into an Emotionally Mature Adult." Use the space provided to answer the Questions to Consider and/or to journal your thoughts each day.

Day 1 Questions to Consider:

What is one step you can take to place yourself (with all your flaws) in the hands of Jesus, inviting him to mold you into a spiritually and emotionally mature disciple?

How can you "practice the presence of people," within an awareness of his presence today?

Day 2 Questions to Consider:

Which words from Henri Nouwen's quotation about the prodigal son speak to you?

What is the biggest challenge you face in being still before the Lord?

Day 3 Questions to Consider:

How can you begin to see Jesus Christ in the people you meet this week?

Take a few moments and consider the people you will encounter today. What might it look like for you to slow down and treat each one as a "Thou" rather than an "It"?

Day 4 Questions to Consider:

What sometimes distracts you from seeing the people you are with as they really are?

What might be one way you can let go of power and control, and, in love, choose to serve someone today?

Day 5 Questions to Consider:

Is there someone God is calling you to stop judging? What might it look like to bless and extend mercy to them?

Where are you experiencing tensions in relationships that you are afraid to disrupt?

Go the Next Step
to Develop
a "Rule of Life"

(90 MINUTES)

Introduction

If we are to nurture a heart that treats every person, ourselves included, as a "Thou" instead of an "It," we need to be intentional about our lives. By ordering our lives to contemplate the love of Christ and to receive the love of Christ, we will be able to give the love of Christ away to others. In this way, he transforms our lives into a gift to our families, friends, coworkers, and communities.

The problem again, however, is our busyness and lack of intentionality. Often, we find ourselves unfocused, distracted, and spiritually adrift. Few of us have a conscious plan for intentionally developing our spiritual lives.

Nurturing a growing spirituality in our present-day culture calls for a thoughtful, conscious, purposeful plan. To do this well requires us to uncover another ancient buried treasure — a "Rule of Life."

Growing Connected (10 minutes)

1. Before we launch fully into our final session, it is important that we pause and consider the past seven sessions:

   - The Problem of Emotionally Unhealthy Spirituality
     (Saul — emotionally unaware and not cultivating his relationship with God)

   - Know Yourself That You May Know God
     (David — courageously living out of his true self)

   - Going Back in Order to Go Forward
     (Joseph — transformed by a very difficult past)

   - Journey through the Wall
     (Abraham — trusting God in a "dark night of the soul")

   - Enlarge Your Soul through Grief and Loss
     (Jesus in Gethsemane — embracing God's will)

   - Discover the Rhythms of the Daily Office and Sabbath
     (Daniel — anchoring himself in God)

   - Grow into an Emotionally Mature Adult
     (The Good Samaritan — modeling an "I-Thou" heart to others)

In light of how God has been coming to you throughout these sessions, complete the following sentence (and then briefly share with the group as time permits):

I am beginning to realize ...

VIDEO: Go the Next Step to Develop a "Rule of Life" (13 minutes)

Watch the video segment for Session 8. Use the space provided to note anything that stands out to you.

NOTES

Group Discussion (22 minutes)

Starters (10 minutes)

2. **Two-Minute Takeaway:** What impacted you most about the video teaching for this session?

3. Take about 5 minutes to think about your life in terms of prayer, rest, work/activity, and relationships. In each box, write one specific thing you are currently doing in each of these four areas to nurture your relationship with Jesus. Then briefly take turns sharing your "nurture" habits with the group.

Prayer	Rest
Work/Activity	Relationships

Bible Study: Acts 2:42 – 47 (12 minutes)

Have a volunteer(s) read the introductory paragraph and Scripture passage, and then discuss the questions that follow.

The Rule of Life will be introduced as we study the first Christian community in the book of Acts. The word *rule* comes from the Greek word for "trellis." A trellis is a tool that enables a grapevine to get off the ground and grow upward, becoming more fruitful and productive. In the same way, a Rule of Life is a trellis that helps us abide in Christ and become more fruitful spiritually.[5] Read Acts 2:42 – 47:

> [42] They devoted themselves to the apostles' teaching and to fellowship, to the breaking of bread and to prayer. [43] Everyone was filled with awe at the many wonders and signs performed by the apostles. [44] All the believers were together and had everything in common. [45] They sold property and possessions to give to anyone who had need. [46] Every day they continued to meet together in the temple courts. They broke bread in their homes and ate together with glad and sincere hearts, [47] praising God and enjoying the favor of all the people. And the Lord added to their number daily those who were being saved.

4. In the book of Acts, we are given a window into the life of the first community of believers soon after the coming of the Holy Spirit at Pentecost when three thousand people came to faith in Christ. What speaks to you from this passage?

5. Based on this one passage, how would you describe this community's Rule of Life? Describe the activities/disciplines they used to grow and mature in Christ.

Application and Closing Prayer (45 minutes)

Read the introductory paragraphs and answer question 6 on your own (20 minutes), and then follow the instructions provided for questions 7 and 8 before closing the study in prayer.

Now it is time for you to begin developing your own personal Rule of Life. The following story and questions are meant to help you discern what may be getting in the way of developing a way of life that keeps you closely connected to God.

In his book *A Hidden Wholeness*,[6] Parker Palmer relates a story about farmers in the Midwest who would prepare for blizzards by tying a rope from the back door of their house out to the barn as a guide to ensure they could return safely home. These blizzards came quickly and fiercely and were highly dangerous. When their full force was blowing, a farmer could not see the end of his or her hand. Many froze to death in those blizzards, disoriented by their inability to see. They wandered in circles, lost sometimes in their own backyards. If they lost their grip on the rope, it became impossible for them to find their way home. Some froze within feet of their own back door, never realizing how close they were to safety.

Many of us are wandering amidst the blizzards of life and have lost our way spiritually.

6. Spend time alone with God around the following questions:

  • What is the nature of your blizzard at this time?

  • What contributes to your blizzard? What does it look like? Feel like?

  • What does that blizzard obscure? What gets "lost"?

- We each need a rope to keep us connected to God. Notice that every rope is actually made up of a series of smaller, intertwined threads. In light of your life at this time, what "threads" do you want to make up your rope (Rule of Life)?

7. After your time alone, get into groups of two. Share what you discovered in your time alone. (10 minutes)

8. Gather as a large group and invite those who would like to share how God is coming to them regarding the blizzard and their own personal "Rule of Life." (10 minutes)

As a group, spend time in prayer, giving thanks to God for your time both in the group and for the new things God is doing in your journey with him. (5 minutes)

Personal Study for the Coming Days

 Read Week 8 of *Emotionally Healthy Spirituality Day by Day*, "Grow into an Emotionally Healthy Adult." Use the space provided to answer the Questions to Consider and/or to journal your thoughts each day.

Day 1 Questions to Consider:

What is your plan, in the midst of your busy day, for not leaving the nurturing of your interior life with God to chance?

How and why do you think finding time alone with God in silence might "teach you everything"?

Day 2 Questions to Consider:

What spoke to you when you read about the lifestyle of the early Christians in Acts and the way they sought to follow the life of Jesus?

Where can you find the time in your week to "gaze on the infinite beauty of God"?

Day 3 Questions to Consider:

What difference might it make if you were to practice "building open spaces" into your life?

In what ways might God be searching for you today — knocking on the door of your life?

Day 4 Questions to Consider:

What might it look like for you to "run on the path of God's commandments"?

What lines from Patrick's prayer speak to you? Carry them in your heart today.

Day 5 Questions to Consider:

What fears are you carrying that you can release to your Abba Father today?

What might it look like for God's love to invade and fill you, guiding you to what you must do?

Leader's Guide

Overview of the Course

The *Emotionally Healthy Spirituality* (*EHS*) *Course*, of which this workbook is a part, provides an indispensable foundation to integrate the larger, deeper, beneath-the-surface spiritual formation paradigm of Emotionally Healthy Spirituality into the life of your church.

At New Life Fellowship Church and churches around the world, we realized that this content — more than just an elective small group curriculum — was so critical that it needed to be offered two to three times a year. Why? First, we wanted every newcomer and member to grasp our core values around spiritual formation. Second, we wanted to ensure the long-term integration of Emotionally Healthy Spirituality into every aspect of the church. The radical, introductory call of discipleship found in the *EHS Course* serves as both an entry point and an essential bridge into the larger EHS vision. For more information, go to www.emotionallyhealthy.org.

General Guidelines

1. Be sure to preview the video segment and read the related workbook content before each session. Becoming familiar with the material and instructions will allow you to comfortably lead your group. You will also want to read the corresponding chapter(s) in the *Emotionally Healthy Spirituality* book before each session.

2. Have copies of this workbook, the *Emotionally Healthy Spirituality* book, and the *Emotionally Healthy Day by Day* devotional available for each participant to purchase at the first two sessions. Make scholarships available, if possible, for those who need financial

assistance. Though a person can participate in the group without reading the book and devotional, reading the recommended content tends to make for a deeper transformational impact — and thus is highly recommended.

3. Each session — a combination of video presentation and discussion, group and individual activities, and prayer — will require 90 minutes to complete. The first meeting, however, may take an additional 20 – 30 minutes because it lays the foundation for the other sessions. Respect everyone by beginning and ending on time.

4. Set up the meeting room in a way that will comfortably seat all participants, preferably in a circle so that everyone can see each other. Arrive at least 15 minutes ahead of time to test your video player to be sure that it is working properly and to greet group members individually as they come in.

5. To kick off each meeting, you may want to read aloud the Introduction found at the beginning of that session of the workbook (it is also found in the video presentation). Then follow the workbook's instructions section by section for the remainder of the session. And be sure to encourage participants to take advantage of the Personal Study reading and journaling opportunities between sessions.

6. The nature of this material easily lends itself to lengthy sharing. One of your greatest challenges as the group leader/facilitator will be to keep the group focused and to share within the time frames allotted for each part of the session. It is important to cover each section of every session in order to give your group broad exposure to each topic as they begin the journey into emotionally healthy spirituality.

7. If your group is large, you may want to break into smaller groups of three to four people so that everyone has a chance to participate.

8. When appropriate, it will be helpful if you lead by example — being vulnerable and open with life examples from your own journey.

9. Remember, we are only experts on *our own* journey. Respect where each person is in their journey with Christ. The Holy Spirit will prompt and lead each person differently and at different paces through this material. Remember that people change slowly — and that includes you!

Additional Suggestions from *Leading Bible Discussions*[7]

1. Avoid answering your own questions. Feel free to rephrase a question until it is clearly understood.

2. Encourage more than one answer to each question. Ask, "What do the rest of you think?" or "Anyone else?"

3. Try to be affirming whenever possible. Let people know you appreciate their contributions.

4. Try not to reject an answer. If it is clearly wrong, ask, "What in the passage led you to that conclusion?"

5. Avoid going off on tangents. If people wander off course, gently bring them back to the subject at hand.

Specific Guidelines for Each Session

SESSION 1: *The Problem of Emotionally Unhealthy Spirituality*

In addition to the general guidelines, here are some other helpful items to note by section:

Before the Session

- Read chapters 1 – 3 of the book *Emotionally Healthy Spirituality*.

Introduction/Growing Connected

- If this is your small group's first meeting, you may want to add an extra 20 – 30 minutes to this session in order to get acquainted and cover the "housekeeping" points — dates, times, and locations the group will be meeting — if you haven't previously done so.

- Have name tags, Bibles, copies of the *Emotionally Healthy Spirituality Course Workbook*, the *Emotionally Healthy Spirituality* book, and *Emotionally Healthy Spirituality Day by Day* devotional available for newcomers.

- Explain your role as leader/facilitator for the group. Let your group know that you won't be lecturing but learning together with them.

- Be sure to read the "Suggested Guidelines for the Group."

- For at least the first session or two, read instructions aloud as indicated in the workbook in order to keep the group moving at the suggested pace.

Starters

- *(Question 4)* Read and be familiar with other examples of the "10 Top Symptoms of Emotionally Unhealthy Spirituality" in chapter 2 of the *Emotionally Healthy Spirituality* book, page 23.

Bible Study

- The command to "totally destroy everything," including women and children, presents a difficult moral and theological problem for the modern reader. Shortly after leaving Egypt, the Israelites "weary and worn out" were attacked by the Amalekites (Exodus 17:8 – 16). After God granted his people victory, he promised to completely destroy the Amalekites from the face of the earth (see also Deuteronomy 25:17 – 18). Now, through Saul, God determines to carry out his threat. You may want to mention three reasons for such a command. First, Israel was functioning as an instrument of God's judgment on a wicked, utterly sinful culture. Second, Israel needed to eliminate all forms of temptation that might corrupt and prevent them from being God's chosen instrument in the world. This drastic action was needed to maintain holiness (Deuteronomy 7:1 – 6; 20:16 – 18). Finally, in Hebrew the phrase "totally destroy" means "to devote to Yahweh." The spoils, then, were surrendered and dedicated to God and were in some way a sacrifice to God. Be careful not to spend much time on this point.
- *(Question 6)* For those who have not read the book, you will want to explain the iceberg illustration found on pages 15 – 16 of chapter 1 of *Emotionally Healthy Spirituality*.

SESSION 2: *Know Yourself That You May Know God*

In addition to the general guidelines, here are some other helpful items to note by section:

Before the Session

- Read chapter 4 of the book *Emotionally Healthy Spirituality*.

Introduction/Growing Connected

- Have name tags, Bibles, copies of the *Emotionally Healthy Spirituality Course Workbook*, the *Emotionally Healthy Spirituality* book, and *Emotionally Healthy Spirituality Day by Day* devotional available for newcomers.

- Introduce today's topic by mentioning that in the last session, the group looked at Saul and the problem of emotionally unhealthy spirituality. But this week we will look at David and the first principle of emotionally healthy spirituality — knowing ourselves that we may know God.

- You may want to read aloud the "Suggested Guidelines for the Group" again.

- You may want to read instructions aloud as indicated in the workbook, or when appropriate, in order to keep the group moving at the suggested pace.

- *(Question 1)* When people share about their dream job, be aware that it can very often give you (and them) a glimpse of their "true self" in surprising ways.

Starters

- You may want to reread the section "Discovering God's Will and Your Emotions" in *Emotionally Healthy Spirituality* (pages 73 – 74) for a brief summary of the role of feelings in discerning God's will.

- *(Questions 3 – 4)* This exercise may bring up significant pain in some of the members of the group (*ex.:* unresolved anger, sadness that has not been grieved, shame that has been masked). Remember that this is a limited exercise with one goal — to help people *begin* to be aware of how much is going on inside of them. This is not the time to fix or give advice. Giving people space to express their feelings is a gift enough. If "Pandora's box" opens for a member of the group, thank the person for their awareness and vulnerability and let them know that you would be glad to talk with them after the meeting, if they would like. It is important to recognize your role is facilitator/small group leader and not professional counselor. In some cases, you may want to direct them to get the help they need beyond the limits of your group.

Bible Study

- *(Question 9)* One very helpful way to clarify this process of growing into our true selves in a new way is through use of a new term: differentiation. It refers to a person's capacity to "define his or her own life's goals and values apart from the pressures of those around them." The key emphasis of differentiation is the ability to think clearly and carefully as another means, besides our feelings, of knowing ourselves.

    It involves the ability to separate who you are from who you are not. The degree to which you are able to affirm your distinct values and goals apart from the pressures around you (separateness), while remaining close to people important to you (togetherness), helps determine your level of differentiation. People who are highly differentiated — such as David in this Bible account — can choose how they want to behave without being controlled by the approval or disapproval of others. Intensity of feelings, high stress, or the anxiety of others around them does not overwhelm their capacity to think intelligently.

SESSION 3: *Going Back in Order to Go Forward*

In addition to the general guidelines, here are some other helpful items to note by section:

Before the Session

- Read chapter 5 of the book *Emotionally Healthy Spirituality*.

Bible Study

- *(Question 6)* There is no way we can know for sure why Joseph weeps, but numerous possibilities exist. Perhaps he weeps because he knows that Jacob never left instructions that he should not harm the brothers. Maybe he realizes that they will never really change; they are still lying. Or it could be that they are finally admitting their terrible cruelty and sins against Joseph, and Joseph is weeping because his pain is finally validated or acknowledged. It could be that these are tears of joy as he realizes this is the fulfillment of his dream from Genesis 37, or that all the pain of his life has led to the truth of this moment where he must make a momentous decision of whether or not to forgive.

Application

- *(Question 9)* Encourage those who may have done work on their family of origin in some other setting, or even filled out the chart prior to the group meeting, to prayerfully ponder this exercise again. God often surprises us with fresh insights when we have space to contemplate these messages before him.

SESSION 4: *Journey through the Wall*

In addition to the general guidelines, here are some other helpful items to note by section:

Before the Session

- Read chapter 6 of the book *Emotionally Healthy Spirituality*.

Starters

- *(Question 3)* It usually takes a while (sometimes a long while!) to share about a Wall in a person's life. In light of having less than 15 minutes for this question, you as leader/facilitator may want to use the time to share about a Wall that *you* have experienced. We have found that a well-thought out testimony can sometimes be better than open sharing at this point. At the very least, only one or two people will have time to share.

Bible Study

- *(Question 7)* We often carry within us inaccurate beliefs, or ideas, about God. For example, we understand "Take delight in the LORD and he will give you the desires of your heart" (Psalm 37:4) to mean that if we are doing all we think God wants, then only good things will follow. The problem is that this contradicts other Scriptures such as our text here. Abraham was, as far as Scripture indicates, doing God's will. Yet it surely was not the desire of Abraham's heart to kill his son! Job is another classic example. He is an innocent sufferer — what makes his life so bewildering is the undeserved nature of his pain. The principle that we reap what we sow (Galatians 6:7 – 8) did not apply to Job, as his friends argued in Job chapters 3 – 37. For this reason, embracing our Walls frequently results in a crisis of faith for many believers rather than a doorway to transformation.

SESSION 5: *Enlarge Your Soul through Grief and Loss*

In addition to the general guidelines, here are some other helpful items to note by section:

Before the Session

- Read chapter 7 of the book *Emotionally Healthy Spirituality*.

Bible Study

- *(Question 7)* Jesus' response to his grief and loss stands in sharp contrast to Peter's. Jesus, for example, felt deeply his sorrow and pain. He did not "spin" or spiritualize it away. Jesus openly admitted his grief to those close to him and asked for their support. He repeatedly prayed to his Father for an alternative but finally accepted the Father's "no." We see him move through a process from struggling to accept the Father's will to finally rising up to embrace it.

Application

- *(Question 11)* Two questions frequently come up in relation to grieving.

  1. **How do I know I am grieving or if I should be grieving?**
     One way to know if you are grieving is when you experience some of the following symptoms that normally accompany the stages of grieving — depression, anger, disbelief, yearning, bargaining. On the other hand, if you go through a significant loss but do not experience any of the above feelings, you may need a mature, objective outsider to help you move through the process.

2. **How do I know when I am done grieving?**

   There are many factors that impact the amount of time needed to grieve. For example, the deeper the loss, the more time needed to grieve. The loss felt when a child leaves home and goes off to college is very different from the loss experienced should that child die tragically. Another factor is to respect how God has crafted each of us differently. The time you need and I need may be very different. One key principle is to not censor your emotions that come bubbling up as a result of the loss. Allow yourself, like Jesus and David, to feel them deeply before God. Censoring certain feelings because they are "bad" will only prolong or abort the discipleship process needed for long-term transformation in our lives.

SESSION 6: *Discover the Rhythms of the Daily Office and Sabbath*

In addition to the general guidelines, here are some other helpful items to note by section:

Before the Session

- Read chapter 8 of the book *Emotionally Healthy Spirituality*.

Growing Connected

- *(Question 1)* Be sure not to spend too much time here. Realistically, there is only time for two or three people to share.

Starters

- *(Question 3)* The Daily Office is a learned practice that takes time. For some it will be difficult; for others it will not be long enough. Others will struggle with all their interior noise. Be ready for a wide variety of responses. Hopefully, many will have adjusted comfortably to the rhythm of the Daily Office if they have been doing it since your small group began.

Bible Study

- *(Question 5)* The concept of the Daily Office has a rich history going back to David, Daniel, the Jews during Jesus' time, and the early church. It is the rhythm of stopping to be with God at set times during the day so that we can "practice the presence of God."

Application

- As you move into this section, you might note to the group that God modeled for us working six days and resting one. We have managed to turn our "days off" from work into work days as well, filling them with activities (chores, finishing our "to do" lists, etc.). We don't actually stop to rest, delight, and contemplate God.

SESSION 7: *Grow into an Emotionally Mature Adult*

In addition to the general guidelines, here are some other helpful items to note by section:

Before the Session

- Read chapter 9 of the book *Emotionally Healthy Spirituality*.

Starters

- *(Question 3)* Be aware that this can lead to a lively discussion! The following are examples of possible answers: we often emphasize spiritual productivity and gifts, overlooking troublesome character traits; we equate the knowledge of Scripture to spiritual maturity and ignore emotional immaturity; loving well is much more difficult to measure than doing ministry for God. So be prepared to end this discussion in the time allotted and move on to the next section.

Bible Study

- *(Question 8)* It is important that we maintain the creative tension and healthy balance between self-care and self-giving. Living at either extreme leads us to eventually resent people or ignore those in need around us altogether. The Samaritan stopped to help the hurting man. At the same time, he had the self-awareness and self-respect to recognize his limits and decided to resume his own journey the next day. A healthy balance of self-care and self-giving in our lives is necessary in order to live out an "I-Thou" relationship both toward ourselves and others.

Application

- *(Questions 10 and 11)* Advise participants beforehand to avoid examples of expectations around moral issues or responsibilities (*ex.:* domestic abuse, adultery, parent's role in nurturing children, financial integrity in the church). These issues go beyond the scope of this exercise.

SESSION 8: *Go the Next Step to Develop a "Rule of Life"*

In addition to the general guidelines, here are some other helpful items to note by section:

Before the Session

- Read chapter 10 of the book *Emotionally Healthy Spirituality*.

Bible Study

- Please note that this Bible Study section is intentionally only 12 minutes. We have placed the weight of this final meeting on the application exercise and closing prayer, which require 45 minutes.
- *(Question 5)* Notice that there is no hint of legalism or "shoulds" in the description of the church in Acts. Jesus said, "Come to me, all you who are weary … My yoke is easy and my burden is light" (Matthew 11:28 – 30). In the same way, any healthy Rule of Life we develop needs to fit how God made us at this particular season of our life.

Application

- This exercise is best done when participants are given physical space to be alone. If space allows, have the individual members find a personal spot where they can spend these 20 minutes in solitude contemplating the questions before God.

Notes

1. For a more complete understanding of what we mean by emotional health and contemplative spirituality, see the book *Emotionally Healthy Spirituality*, 45 – 46.

2. See *Emotionally Healthy Spirituality*, 45 – 46.

3. For a fuller discussion of Martin Buber's distinction between "I-It" and "I-Thou" relationships, see *Emotionally Healthy Spirituality*, 181 – 183.

4. This exercise is adapted from Pat Ennis, *The Third Option: An Ongoing Program to Build Better Marriages*, Teachers Manual, Topic #3, "Expectations," 1 – 9.

5. Remember, a Rule of Life is simply an intentional, conscious plan to keep God at the center of everything we do. It provides guidelines to help us continually remember God as the source of our lives. It includes our unique combination of spiritual practices that provide structure and direction for us to intentionally pay attention and remember God in everything we do.

6. Parker Palmer, *A Hidden Wholeness* (San Francisco: Jossey-Bass, 2009).

7. James F. Nyquist and Jack Kuhatschek, *Leading Bible Discussions* (Downers Grove, Ill.: InterVarsity Press, 1985).

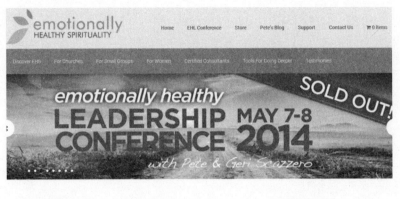

For more information on implementing
Emotionally Healthy Spirituality and
Emotionally Healthy Spirituality Day by Day
into your life, small group, or church, go to:

www.emotionallyhealthy.org

Emotionally Healthy Spirituality

It's Impossible to Be Spiritually Mature, While Remaining Emotionally Immature

Peter Scazzero

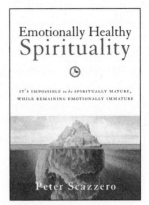

Peter Scazzero learned the hard way: you can't be spiritually mature while remaining emotionally immature. Even though he was a pastor of a growing church, he did what most people do:

- avoided conflict in the name of Christianity
- ignored his anger, sadness, and fear
- used God to run from God
- lived without boundaries

Eventually God awakened him to a biblical integration of emotional health, a relationship with Jesus, and the classic practices of contemplative spirituality. It created nothing short of a spiritual revolution, utterly transforming him and his church.

In this bestselling book Scazzero outlines his journey and the signs of emotionally unhealthy spirituality. He then goes on to provide seven biblical, reality-tested ways to break through to the revolutionary life Christ meant for you. "The combination of emotional health and contemplative spirituality," he says, "unleashes the Holy Spirit inside us so that we might experientially know the power of an authentic life in Christ."

Available in stores and online!

Emotionally Healthy Spirituality Day by Day

A 40-Day Journey with the Daily Office

Peter Scazzero

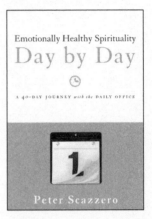

In this groundbreaking devotional book, Peter Scazzero introduces the ancient spiritual discipline of the Daily Office. The basic premise of the Daily Office is simple: We need to intentionally stop to be with God more than once a day so that practicing the presence of God becomes real in our lives.

Each day offers two Daily Offices—Morning/Midday and Midday/Evening—where each pause can last from five to twenty minutes.

Available in stores and online!

The Emotionally Healthy Woman

Eight Things You Have to Quit to Change Your Life

Geri Scazzero with Peter Scazzero

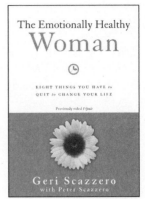

Geri Scazzero knew there was something desperately wrong with her life. She felt like a single parent raising her four young daughters alone. She finally told her husband, "I quit," and left the thriving church he pastored, beginning a journey that transformed her and her marriage for the better.

In *The Emotionally Healthy Woman*, Geri provides you a way out of an inauthentic, superficial spirituality to genuine freedom in Christ. This book is for every woman who thinks, "I can't keep pretending everything is fine!"

The journey to emotional health begins by quitting. Geri quit being afraid of what others think. She quit lying. She quit denying her anger and sadness. She quit living someone else's life. When you quit those things that are damaging to your soul or the souls of others, you are freed up to choose other ways of being and relating that are rooted in love and lead to life.

When you quit for the right reasons, at the right time, and in the right way, you're on the path not only to emotional health, but also to the true purpose of your life.

> *"QUITTING WILL SET YOU FREE!*
>
> *Not a typical message heard in the church today, especially among 'nice, Christian women,' but one that has been needed for years! By refusing to cling to a shell of pretension, the true freedom of our new lives in Christ is realized, and Geri shows us how. A fast, informed read, this book breaks down the walls of the false ideals we cling to in and shows us that by quitting these idols, we rediscover God's love. I was supposed to read this book. I needed to read this book. Thank you, Geri."*
>
> Kim de Blecourt, Short-term Adventure Specialist with
> Food for Orphans and author of *Until We All Come Home:*
> *A Harrowing Journey, a Mother's Courage, a Race to Freedom*

The Emotionally Healthy Woman Workbook

Eight Things You Have to Quit to Change Your Life

Geri Scazzero with Peter Scazzero

Geri Scazzero knew there was something desperately wrong with her life. She felt like a single parent raising her four young daughters alone. She finally told her husband, "I quit," and left the thriving church he pastored, beginning a journey that transformed her and her marriage for the better.

In this eight-session video-based Bible study (DVD sold separately), Geri provides you a way out of an inauthentic, superficial spirituality to genuine freedom in Christ. This study is for every woman who thinks, "I can't keep pretending everything is fine!"

The journey to emotional health begins by quitting. Geri quit being afraid of what others think. She quit lying. She quit denying her anger and sadness. She quit living someone else's life. When you quit those things that are damaging to your soul or the souls of others, you are freed up to choose other ways of being and relating that are rooted in love and lead to life.

When you quit for the right reasons, at the right time, and in the right way, you're on the path not only to emotional health, but also to the true purpose of your life.

Sessions include:

1. Quit Being Afraid of What Others Think
2. Quit Lying
3. Quit Dying to the Wrong Things
4. Quit Denying Anger, Sadness, and Fear
5. Quit Blaming
6. Quit Overfunctioning
7. Quit Faulty Thinking
8. Quit Living Someone Else's Life

The Emotionally Healthy Church,
Expanded Edition

A Strategy for Discipleship That Actually Changes Lives

Peter Scazzero with Warren Bird

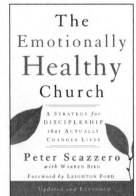

The Emotionally Healthy Church, Updated and Expanded Edition, features a fuller, deeper look at the six principles contained in the original and includes a crucial, additional chapter: Slow Down to Lead with Integrity. New Life Fellowship in Queens, New York, had it all: powerful teaching, dynamic ministries, an impressive growth rate, and a vision to do great works for God. Things looked good—but beneath the surface, circumstances were more than just brewing. They were about to boil over, forcing Peter Scazzero to confront needs in his church and himself that went deeper than he'd ever imagined. What he learned about the vital link between emotional health, relational depth, and spiritual maturity can shed new light on painful problems in your own church. In this revised and expanded edition of his Gold Medallion Award-winning book and groundbreaking bestseller, Scazzero reveals exactly how the truth can and does make you free—not just superficially, but deep down. You'll acquire knowledge and tools that can help you and others:

- look beneath the surface of problems
- break the power of past wounds, failures, sins, and circumstances
- live a life of brokenness and vulnerability
- recognize and honor personal limitations and boundaries
- embrace grief and loss
- make incarnation your model to love others
- slow down to lead with integrity

The Emotionally Healthy Church, Updated and Expanded Edition, includes story after story of people at New Life whose lives have been changed by the concepts in this book.